Hope
and
Help

For a Mother's Heart

CAROL HOPSON

What Readers say about Carol's Books!

Please keep writing Carol! Your books have reached my heart like no others and I read a lot. I think it's because they're so practical and they have so much Scripture in them.   Sue

My wife had me read your book when I had become so discouraged and defeated in life. Praise God, it was exactly what I needed. When I decided to make right choices, I began to see the light again and God has healed me and our marriage.   Tom

I've never read a book that touched my heart so specifically as yours. It was like you were living in my skin and I couldn't believe what I was reading. Thank you for showing me the way back to the Lord. I can't wait to share your book with my family and friends.

Alice

When the bottom fell out of our lives we didn't know where to turn. Someone handed us your first two books and the titles grabbed us. We were in Christian Ministry and had been devastated by rumors and unjust situations. You have to know that God used your books in profound ways to help us through a very difficult time. Thank you, thank you, thank you, for your transparency and faithfulness to the Lord.

A Minister

I love all the poetry in your books. They are so insightful and express just what I'm feeling. I read them over and over for encouragement.   Mimi

I didn't realize how bitter and angry I had become until I read "But God, This Wasn't My Plan!" It literally saved my life! As I chose the

path of obedience and chose to believe all the truths from God's Word that you included in your book, my whole perspective changed. Now I'm living victoriously! I'm forever grateful that you shared your story.

Jan

After I read "My Day, His Way" I was so inspired to start giving each day to the Lord and be available wherever I am. It changed my total outlook on life and now I can't wait to see what God will do each day. Thank you, thank you for your life and books.

Amy

The "Facing Fear with Faith" chapter was exactly what I needed. Thank you for being so honest and giving me so much of God's Word to cling to.
Karen

I was so tired of waiting for people and things to change. I really had given up because life just didn't make sense to me anymore. Then I read your book and the tears began to flow. I realized I was telling God what to do rather than being His servant. Your "Waiting" book changed my outlook completely and now I'm focused on pleasing Him and leaving my situation with Him.

Natalie

Your "Peace in the Midst" book has touched so many lives in our church. We used it for a Women's Bible Study and the result was a newly committed group of women who are so excited about choosing God's peace each day.
Joy

"And He put a new song in my mouth, a song of praise to our God; many will see it and fear and trust in the Lord."

Psalm 40:3

TABLE OF CONTENTS

INTRODUCTION

If only I would have done things differently...

If only my child would listen to me...

If only I knew what to do with this child...

If only my husband would be more involved...

If only my kids were like my friend's kids...

If only my kids wouldn't fight so much...

If only I didn't get so angry...

If only the divorce could have been prevented...

If only my child would return to the Lord...

If only my kids would make better choices...

If only I could start over...

Do you recognize any of these statements? I don't think you'd be normal if you didn't identify with one or more of these. However, this kind of thinking only leads to pain, guilt, frustration and discouragement. The reason for this book is to help you, a precious, imperfect mother of a precious imperfect child, find peace, joy, purpose and hope.

This is a brand new day...a fresh start! The God Who created you and your child, Who parted the Red Sea, Who calmed the storm, Who raised the dead, is certainly able to do the impossible in you and for you. As you turn the pages of this book and begin this new journey with the Savior, why not ask Him to forgive your past mistakes...we've all made them. Ask Him to take His living

Word from these pages and heal your heart, change your focus, give you hope and restore your joy as His beloved child. Go on, don't just think about it, do it! Would you believe that He wants that more than you do?

"And so Lord, where do I put my hope?
My only hope is in You."
"I wait quietly before God, for my hope is in Him."
"This hope we have as an anchor of the soul…"
Psalm 39:7, 62:5a, NLT
Hebrews 6:19a

To anchor your soul in the Savior, read on!

PLEASE NOTE THAT THERE ARE
BIBLE STUDY QUESTIONS FOR EACH CHAPTER
AT THE END OF THIS BOOK.

ON MOTHERHOOD
(for mothers of imperfect children)

At times a mother wonders if her children ever know
The time, the love, the sacrifice that on them she bestows.

Through all her years she willingly gives them her very best
And prays that God who loves them so will take care of the rest.

Sometimes it's disappointing to see the choices made
And all her hopes and dreams for them seem to so quickly fade.

Sometimes it's never-ending, the prayers for them at night
When she knows they are struggling to do what's best and right.

Sometimes it seems a thankless job, at other times it's great.
And no two kids are quite alike, to each she must relate.

The task is overwhelming, bringing pain and also pleasure,
But what is done in Jesus' name is what the Lord will measure.

So let the love of Jesus flow freely out through you.
And love them just the way they are and not for what they do.

For that's the way our Father loves, how thankful we should be
That His love isn't measured by the good or bad He sees.

So as you go about your day, throw expectations out.
Give up those disappointments that make you want to pout.

And thank God for His blessings, His mercy and His grace,
Then let Him fill your heart with joy, as each new day you face.

Carol Hopson

Chapter One

The Sacrifices of Motherhood

"At times a mother wonders if her children ever know,
The time, the love, the sacrifice that on them she bestows."

Yes, motherhood is full of sacrifices; we sacrifice our sleep, our bodies, our personal time, our hobbies and sometimes our dreams…all because of our love for our children.

- Sometimes it's easy, we feel so proud and happy to be a mom!

- Sometimes we feel suffocated, as we realize someone always needs something from us.

- Sometimes we feel angry, thinking, "I have no time to do what I want to do!"

- Sometimes we feel discouraged, with thoughts like, "I'm a terrible mother; these children don't have a chance!"

- Sometimes we think, "God made a mistake when he made me a mother."

Ah yes, the thoughts of a busy mother can lead to all sorts of conclusions. But, does God have any words for the mom who gives so much of herself? Does He care about her sacrifices? Will it be worth it all in the end?

First of all, let me remind you that God knows about sacrifices. Remember that He gave His only Son to pay the price for all your failures, mistakes and sinful choices. (John 3:16-18) He also knows your heart. He is fully aware of your situation and your life. You are one of His precious sheep.

"O Lord, you have examined my heart and know everything about me.

You know when I sit down or stand up.

You know my every thought when far away.

You chart the path ahead of me and tell me where to stop and rest.

Every moment you know where I am.

You know what I am going to say even before I say it, Lord.

You both precede and follow me.

You place your hand of blessing on my head.

Such knowledge is too wonderful for me, too great for me to know!"

(Psalm 139:1-6 New Living Translation)

So how does this bring comfort to a mother who sacrifices so much? Because God knows how you feel and He is the only One who truly understands your needs and emotions. You are one of His precious children and He hurts when you hurt. My children are now married with children of their own and yet that same pain penetrates my heart when I hear that they are troubled or hurting. I feel their hurt in a very real way and want to do all I can to help them.

Sometimes that means I do something specific, sometimes I send a word of encouragement, sometimes I just listen, sometimes

I offer advice, but always I pray. My response is different in each situation but my love is always the same. That's the way it is with our Heavenly Father. He is always loving us even though we can't always understand it, just the way you and I will always love our children. Think of that the next time you feel overworked and under-appreciated.

He revealed to me that I was choosing to set the guidelines for how and when I would sacrifice for Him.

He knows what your day is like and He will give you the ability to accomplish **what He wants you to accomplish** in the day as you seek His priorities for your day. One of the main reasons we don't seek His priorities is because our eyes have turned inward. Just in the last month, I had surgery for cancer on my leg, had six new crowns put in my mouth in one morning, threw a surprise dinner for thirty people for my husband's birthday, began a new Mom's Bible study and was committed to speak at retreats every weekend for a month. Each time I left to speak, my mouth hurt (I had over 10 canker sores in my mouth from the oral work), my leg hurt (from eighteen stitches) and I was tired of being in pain. One night I just felt overwhelmed and wondered why I was feeling so low. As I waited on the Lord for an answer, He revealed to me that I was choosing to set the guidelines for how and when I would sacrifice for Him. That is not truly sacrifice. He had allowed my health problems and was fully aware of when I was speaking for Him.

I recently learned what the deaf sign is for sacrifice, and it truly penetrated my heart. Can you picture your two hands with your fists closed, facing down at waist level. Now, raise your hands upward and release your fists, ending up with your hands wide open and reaching up to heaven. If you do it quickly, it is like thrusting something heavenward. Dear mothers, that is exactly what we need to do with our children and our own "needs." **We must let go of the "what ifs" and "if onlys" and throw them up to our Heavenly Father because we love Him more than we love our own way.** Then our hearts are ready to receive the incredible joy that He will give us as we choose to walk in obedience and acceptance of His plan, not ours.

It all gets down to trust. Who do we trust, ourselves or our Savior? When Paul was in prison he wrote, "*I know the One in whom I trust, and I am sure that He is able to guard what I have entrusted to Him…*" (2 Timothy 1:12). To entrust the Lord with our children, our sacrifices, our "if onlys," means that we put everything in His hands and leave it there. When my kids leave their children in my care, they don't stand at the door and open it every five minutes asking, "Did you remember to feed the grandchildren? Did you remember to put them down for naps? Are you sure you're giving them your time and love? You see, they trust me because they know how much I love each one of them. How much more then, can we trust the One who gave His life for us!

To entrust the Lord with our children, our sacrifices, our "if onlys," means that we put everything in His hands and leave it there.

Encouragement from God's Heart to Yours!

"I am sure that God, who began the good work within you, will continue his work until it is finally finished on that day when Christ Jesus comes back again."

(Philippians 1:6, NLT)

"He who offers a sacrifice of thanksgiving honors me..."

(Psalm 50:23a)

A sacrifice of thanksgiving is giving up something I love for something or Someone I love more.

"So, my dear brothers and sisters, (that's you) be strong and steady, (don't give up or be discouraged) always enthusiastic about the Lord's work, (the discipline, discipleship and daily care for your children) for you know that nothing you do for the Lord is ever useless" (nothing you do in your daily life as a mother and none of the sacrifices you make, if done as unto Him, are useless).

(1 Corinthians 15:58, NLT. Parenthesis mine).

SURRENDER FROM YOUR HEART TO HIS!

Dear Father:

Please forgive me for getting a martyr complex sometimes. Help me to remember that you have placed me where I am and you will lovingly see me through each day. Please help me remember how much you love me, and help me pass that love on to my children. I ask you to help me take my eyes off of myself and refocus on what you want to accomplish in my life. Thank you for hearing me today and thanks for making the greatest sacrifice of all...giving your Son for me. I love you, Father.

Your Child_____

Bible Study Questions for Chapter One are on page 81.

Chapter Two

The Prayers of Motherhood

❧

"Through all her years she willingly gives them her very best,
And prays that God who loves them so will take care of the rest."

re you a praying mother? I know what you're thinking, "Here comes conviction time!" You probably think this is going to make you feel guilty. On the contrary, I want you to feel excited, encouraged...hopeful! There are so many things in our children's lives that are out of our control and we can easily get so discouraged.

- Sometimes we can't control their actions.
- Sometimes their attitude just stinks!
- Sometimes they make poor choices that have serious consequences.
- Sometimes they lack the convictions that you have tried to teach them.
- Sometimes they disobey over and over and over.

We can't control their actions, but we can control our attitude towards their actions. I know you try to give your best to them, to teach them right from wrong, but there are always those kids who choose to do things their own way. If you have one or more of those, here's where the encouragement comes. When you feel you have no control, go to the One Who is still in control! Determine before God to not let discouragement defeat you. You always have a choice.

We can't control their actions, but we can control our attitude towards their actions.

Recently, I received a phone call that immediately made my heart sink. My attitude went from Hallelujahs to just hanging on! I knew Satan was working overtime and I knew that I had no control to change this situation. Okay Carol, get a grip and remember what God wants you to do. I knew He didn't want me to feel defeated or fearful so I needed to face my fears with the truths of His Word. When your child breaks your heart by his or her choices, your first reaction is such deep pain and discouragement. But what does God want you to do with that pain? He tells you in 1 Thessalonians 5:17, "*Pray without ceasing.*" Pray while cooking, pray while driving (with eyes wide open, of course), pray while waiting in carpool lanes and pray when worries flood your mind in the night. God knew how you would worry and so He gave you and me explicit instructions. "*So humble yourselves under the mighty power of God, and in His good time He will honor you. Give all your worries and cares to God, for He cares about what happens to you.*" (1 Peter 5:6-7, NLT). Are you wondering why you should pray? I'm glad you asked!

Before giving you the answer, let me tell you a story. It seems that God uses the sprinkler system in each of the places where we've lived, to try us and teach us...to try us if we make wrong choices...to teach us if we make right choices. This was no exception! I was home and my husband was away for the day on business. Of course, this was when the new sprinkler system decided to go bonkers and stay on for 8 hours. It flooded the yard, it flooded the bedrooms, it flooded everywhere! I came home to find everything wet and I couldn't get the water to shut off. I tried to flag someone down in the street to help, but to no avail. No neighbors could be reached and now the pipes had broken and water was gushing. I tried over and over and over to reach my husband on his cell phone. He didn't answer and my frustration level grew. He was always reachable by phone, but now when I desperately needed him, he wasn't answering.

After many, many tries, I finally got through to him with my frustration and explained the situation. He calmly told me what to do and said he'd be home in fifteen minutes. It amazed me how I felt after that. I was so relieved all of a sudden. Why was that? I had put the problem in my capable husband's hands; he now knew about the problem and I could trust him to take care of it. What a relief and what a lesson for me! That's exactly how God the Father wants me to feel when I place my frustrating circumstance (or child) in His hands. Let's look at what prayer does for us:

1. <u>Praying puts your focus on the Lord and not on your circumstances.</u>

"*I have set the Lord continually before me; because He is at my right hand, I shall not be greatly shaken.*" (Psalm 16:8). I want to give you another mental picture that you can visualize. Hold your Bible up in front of your eyes and look directly at it. With your other hand, hold up a piece of paper just behind the Bible. The Bible represents God's promises, power and love for you. The paper represents the circumstance or problem you are struggling with. As you set the Bible (God's power) in front of you, you see your problem only through the power of God or you don't see it at all. When worry or fear creeps into your life, it is because you have placed the paper in front of your Bible; you have set your circumstances continually before you and so you are greatly shaken because the problem has replaced God's power and presence in your thinking.

2. <u>Praying correctly aligns your heart with God's heart.</u>

Jesus prayed, *"Father, if Thou art willing, remove this cup from me, yet not My will, but Thine be done."* (Luke 22:42). As a child, I would love to hear my father pray. His voice sounded so reassuring and he seemed to have such a special relationship with God. I always noticed something about his prayers; he always used the phrase "Lord willing" when he asked anything. It was such a natural part of talking to God that it also became a natural part of my prayers. As I grew in my faith and knowledge of the word, I realized that this was the way we get our will in line with God's. We openly tell Him what we think we need and then we ask for His will to be done. A great preacher once said, "Prayer is not to change God, but to change us."

We openly tell Him what we think we need and then we ask for His will to be done.

3. <u>Praying calms your troubled heart.</u>

"Many are the sorrows of the wicked, but he who trusts in the Lord, lovingkindness shall surround him." "I sought the Lord and He answered me and delivered me from all my fears." (Psalm 32:10, 34:4).

My daughter had been hit by a car in front of our house and was lying motionless in the street. Fear raced through my veins and pierced my heart like a sword. I knew I had no strength to handle what was ahead and so I instantly asked God to calm my fearful heart and help me handle whatever He allowed to happen to my precious daughter. With that prayer came an amazing calmness that stayed with me until she was safely delivered to the emergency room and I was safely in my husband's arms. It was a miracle of God's grace to meet my need.

4.   <u>Praying prepares our hearts to receive God's grace.</u>

"Come unto me all who are weary and heaven-laden, and I will give you rest. Take my yoke upon you, and learn from Me, for I am gentle and humble in heart; and you shall find rest for your souls." (Matthew 11:28-29).

I'll never forget a dinner at a large Mexican restaurant when my first granddaughter was barely two-years-old. We lived about two hours from our son and his family and so we had arranged to meet at a restaurant that was halfway between us. Evidently, Monica, our grandchild, didn't know that we were going to be there and when she entered the restaurant and spotted us clear across the room, this quiet, gentle, well-behaved little toddler shrieked "Nana!!" at the top of her lungs, bringing the whole room to attention. Well, my heart leaped with such pride and joy and I got up and swung her up into my arms and smothered her with my love. The entire restaurant seemed to get caught up in the joyful reunion and clapped as they saw the joy in both our faces.

I've often thought that this might be the way the Lord feels when we come to His throne and cry "Abba Father." He is so thrilled that we have come and is so ready to pour out His love and grace upon us. Do you need to feel His loving arms today? Run to Him and tell Him how much you need Him…He's so anxious to show you how much He loves you.

Encouragement from God's Heart to Yours!

"Now may the Lord of peace Himself continually grant you peace in every circumstance; The Lord be with you all!"

(2 Thessalonians 3:16)

"The steadfast of mind Thou wilt keep in perfect peace, because He trusts in Thee."

(Isaiah 26:3)

"My flesh and my heart may fail, but God is the strength of my heart and my portion forever."

(Psalm 73:26)

"When I am afraid, I will put my trust in Thee. In God, whose word I praise, in God I have put my trust; I shall not be afraid. What can mere man do to me?"

(Psalm 56:3-4)

Surrender from Your Heart to His!

Dear Father:

Please forgive me for trying to carry my own burdens. I'm so tired of trying to fix everyone and everything. Please help me to remember that you love my children even more than I do. Thank you for reminding me, through your word, that You are the One in control and only You can bring change in my child's life. Help me to let go and let You work. I pray that I would be a living example to my child of loving and serving you with a joyful heart, and I'll leave all the rest in your loving hands. I love you Father.

Your Child_____

Bible Study Questions for Chapter Two are on page 84.

Hope and Help for a Mother's Heart

Chapter Three

The Dreams of Motherhood

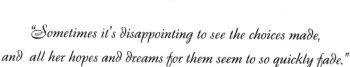

*"Sometimes it's disappointing to see the choices made,
and all her hopes and dreams for them seem to so quickly fade."*

I've never met anyone yet who has told me that all her hopes, plans and dreams have worked out just exactly as she thought they would. Instead, I talk with hundreds of hurting, confused moms who can't understand why God has allowed this or that to happen. I recently counseled a mom whose two children had both turned away from the Lord, making devastating choices. She had literally lived for those children, they were her life. And now, she felt like her life was over, ruined, a failure.

*Could it be that God isn't nearly as interested in
straight A's and athletic prowess as He is in character
and integrity in your child and in you?*

Maybe you're a young mother who thought your child would easily obey, excel in school and have a natural ability for all sports. Okay, maybe you just hoped for one of those but none seem to be a reality. You ask yourself why? Could it be that God isn't nearly as interested in straight A's and athletic prowess as He is in character and integrity in your child and in you? Are you asking God's help to model and teach those important traits? Are you looking for ways to encourage the strengths in your child, especially when they're not what you would have chosen? Are you seeking the Savior's mind?

When my daughter was very young, I found myself trying to get her to be outgoing, the life of the party, the one who steps up and introduces herself and makes everyone her friend. She was only in preschool and yet, I wanted her to have a certain personality that I thought she needed. What I was really doing was trying to make her a little "me." That's the only way I knew for little girls to be happy and successful. I found myself pushing her to be more outgoing and getting frustrated that she was rather quiet and shy. After receiving wise counsel from a friend and from God's Word, I asked forgiveness from the Lord and then went to my precious daughter and asked her forgiveness. I don't think she knew what I was asking but she did begin to see a different mommy from that day on. I began to ask God to show me the traits in her that He had designed for His glory, not the ones I thought were so important.

As I surrendered my idea of what my daughter should be like, the Lord literally opened my eyes to see how He had uniquely created her. (Psalm 139:1-6) She had such a sweet, tender, sensitive heart that responded to one person at a time. Now that she's a mother of three small children, I look back and see how amazingly God has used her quiet, gentle, real spirit to touch others' lives. Over the years, I grew to desire to be more like her as God did such incredibly beautiful things with her personality that, at first, I had tried to change. Praise the Lord, He convicted me and opened my eyes and heart to see how He had created her.

Do you need to ask God to open your eyes to whom your child really is?

Here are some ways to refocus:

- What qualities have I been ignoring because of my limited perspective?

- Have I truly listened to this child with an open heart to hear what is important to him/her?

- Have I tried to open new doors for him or her that are out of my comfort zone? (art, music, science, gymnastics, helping the elderly, volunteering at a hospital, etc.)

- Is there a tender spirit that I need to praise and seek to guide?

- Have I spent time in prayer asking God to give me His wisdom in how to love, encourage and disciple this child? (James 1:5)

- Do I see any of the fruit of the Spirit that could be the basis for character building and fruit-bearing? (Galatians 5:22-23)

- Do I need to ask my child's forgiveness for trying to push him or her into a specific mold?

Your situation might be totally different. Maybe your child has broken your heart and it's not a matter of having different goals and interests, but having a child whose heart has turned away from the Lord. Maybe you have an older child who made a poor choice in marriage. Maybe divorce has crashed into your family and you see all the suffering it has caused. I'm sure you realize that you can't change your children's circumstances by now, but here is what you can do. You can take your broken dreams to your Heavenly Father and accept His plan and loving care for you. Then you can seek to bring His light and love to the situation.

Focusing on broken dreams is destructive because:

1. It hinders us from being all God desires us to be. (Jeremiah 17:5-8)

2. It distorts our perspective regarding our child's possibilities. (Galatians 6:9)

3. It keeps us discouraged and unavailable to respond to God's love and direction. (Psalm 119:11, 27-28, 66-67)

4. It keeps us from putting God's mercy and grace on display in our lives. (Philippians 1:20)

5. It breaks our fellowship with the Lord because we are not being obedient in our thought life. He warns us to think on what is true, honorable, right, pure, lovely and admirable. (Philippians 4:8)

So, if feeling sorry for ourselves because of our broken dreams brings about only negative things in our lives, why do we continue to do it?

I can answer that from my own experience. It happens because I've allowed Satan to confuse me about my purpose. I quickly forget that God's plan and my plan are often not the same, and I get discouraged or even angry. God's plan is that I would "please Him in all respects." Here's our purpose as written in Colossians 1:10: "*We ask God to give you a complete understanding of what He wants to do in your lives, and we ask Him to make you wise with spiritual wisdom. Then the way you live will always honor and please the Lord, and you will continually do good, kind things for others. All the while, you will learn to know God better and better.*" (NLT) I just don't see anything there about our purpose being to dwell on broken dreams or have our way, do you? And you know what? I've learned that I feel so much better when I quickly give up the hurt and ask God to use me in the midst of it, to know Him better and share His love with others.

If you find that your emotions are directly related to the ups and downs of your child's behavior, that is a serious warning sign. Your children can actually become a type of idol in that they are your whole focus in life. They are all you think about, their qualities define you and you judge your day and your worth by their behavior. God is a jealous God (2 Corinthians 11:2) and deserves your love and devotion every day, not just what's left over at the end of the day. He wants to delight in you because you are His workmanship, His beautiful poem, His precious child. (Ephesians 2:10)

If you find that your emotions are directly related to the ups and downs of your child's behavior, that is a serious warning sign.

A dear mother wrote to me after reading my first book, "But God, This Wasn't My Plan!" She had such incredible dreams for her first-born daughter and she had every reason to hope they would come true. Her child had been obedient, loving and seemed to want to live for the Lord. When this dear mother received the call that her daughter was pregnant, she felt like her life was shattered and she could hardly breathe. She writes, "As God used the words in your book and the Scripture verses that you shared, I realized that I had to give up my dreams for what my daughter's life would be like and I began to accept His plan and His love for me. Through my tears of brokenness and submission, He performed a miracle that very night as I surrendered my child and my broken dreams. I can't say it's all been easy, it hasn't! I know that the consequences of sin hurt many, but I also know that God's forgiveness is available to all of us. But God has made something beautiful out of it all. He has restored our fellowship with our daughter, He has brought her a wonderful loving, Christian husband. He has given me a ministry with moms who are going through the same thing that I went through and He has become my source of strength that I had never really known before. But, I had to give up my brokenness before He could do the mending. I realized that I was living my life through my children's choices and not as an individual, separate from my children, as God's beloved child. I hope you'll share my story with others so they will be encouraged and find hope."

Encouragement from God's Heart to Yours!

He will sustain you.

"The Lord sustains all who fall, and raises up all who are bowed down."

(Psalm 145:14)

He will uphold you and hold your hand.

"For I am the Lord your God, who upholds your right hand, Who says to you, 'Do not fear, I will help you.'"

(Isaiah 41:13)

He will strengthen you and help you.

"Do not fear, for I am with you; do not anxiously look about you, for I am your God. I will strengthen you, surely I will help you, surely I will uphold you with My righteous right hand."

(Isaiah 41:10)

He will help you know what to do moment by moment.

"I will instruct you and teach you in the way which you should go; I will counsel you with My eye upon you."

(Psalm 32:8)

He will give you His peace.

"Peace I leave with you; My peace I give to you; not as the world gives, do I give to you. Let not your heart be troubled."

(John 14:27)

Surrender from Your Heart to His!

Dear Father:

I realize that hanging on to my dreams has only made me bitter and frustrated. I know you love me and my child, and you must hurt too when you see the choices we've all made. Please help me to forgive myself and my child for the wrong and hurtful choices. Help me to lay aside my dreams and put my eyes on You and your faithfulness. Open my eyes to see what you might be doing to bring about your character in me. Help me remember that I am separate from my children and can make choices that please and glorify You each day. I ask that you would mend my broken dreams and bring something beautiful out of this, for Your glory. And, may I be available to be a light for you in the midst of it all. I love you Father.

Your Child_____

Bible Study Questions for Chapter Three are on page 87.

Chapter Four

The Struggle of Motherhood

❧

*"Sometimes it's never-ending, the prayers for them at night,
when she knows they are struggling, to do what's best and right."*

You've seen the struggle…he knows he shouldn't hit his brother but he decides to do it anyway. She knows she shouldn't date an unbeliever but she sneaks out to be with him. You know you shouldn't lose your temper but…uh oh, maybe I'm getting too personal. We all struggle with making the right choices; even the apostle Paul said, "…*the trouble is not with the law but with me, because I am sold into slavery, with sin as my master. I don't understand myself at all, for I really want to do what is right, but I don't do it. Instead, I do the very thing I hate.*" (Romans 7:14)

So, knowing how difficult it is, how can we help our children make good choices that honor the Lord? First, we can do specific things with them and secondly, we can pray specific things for them.

What we can do:

1. Spend time praying with them each morning before they go off to school. (Doesn't need to be long.)

2. <u>Give them a verse to think on</u> for the day or week. (Put it on a 3x5 card and encourage them to share with you how it helped them or convicted them at the end of the day.)

3. <u>Give positive reinforcement for good choices</u>, especially in small day-to-day things. ("I noticed how you let your sister get into the car first. That was very thoughtful of you and I really appreciate it.")

4. <u>Start early with appropriate consequences</u> for wrong choices.

5. <u>Share your own personal struggles</u> and how you ask God to help you make good choices that please Him. Tell them how that makes you feel.

6. <u>Try to work on inward conviction with your child, rather than just outward conformity</u>. (This teaching involves the motives of the heart and your concern for their maturity and growth. Seeking only outward conformity is concerned with "how my child looks" to others.)

7. <u>Use their bedtime as an opportunity to talk</u> about their day. This is one of the most valuable times in your relationship with your children...at all ages! Don't let the communication gap happen in your home! Here are some good questions to begin with:

    a. What good choice did you make today?

    b. Did anything make you sad today?

    c. What wrong choice did you make and how could you handle it differently the next time?

    d. What was the most difficult thing in your day?

    e. What would you like me to pray for right now?

    f. What did you do that might have caused Jesus to smile today?

    g. If you could change anything about your day, what would it be?

How We Can Pray for Our Children:

Dr. Joe White, in his book entitled "Faith Training," gives the following helpful list of what we need to pray for:

1. Pray that nothing will hinder your children from accepting Christ as their personal Savior early in life. (Matthew 18:6; 19:14)

2. Pray that your children will learn to know their God, and will have a deep desire to do His will for their lives. (Psalm 119:27, 30, 34-35)

3. Pray that as your children hear stories from the Bible, a genuine love for God and His Word will become such a part of their lives that it will be the basis for all their decision making throughout life. (Psalm 71:17; Ecclesiastes 12:1; 2 Timothy 3:15)

4. Pray that your children will develop a keen sense of what's right and wrong, that they will truly abhor evil and cling to that which is good. (Psalm 51:10, 139:23-24; Romans 12:9)

5. Pray that your kids will increase in wisdom mentally, in stature physically, and in favor with God spiritually, and with man socially. (Luke 2:52)

6. Pray that your children will develop a thankful heart and a fine, confident mental attitude. (Psalm 126:2-3; Romans 8:31)

7. Pray that God will protect your kids from Satan and his wiles in every area of their lives. (Psalm 121:8; John 17:15)

8. Pray that God will destroy the enemies in your children's lives, whatever they may be…weaknesses, lying, selfishness, disobedience and so on. (Psalm 120:2; Philippians 2:4)

9. Pray that God will make your kids successful in the work He has planned for them to do. (Psalm 118:25; 139:9-10)

10. Pray that your kids will respect those in authority over them. (Romans 13:1; Ephesians 6:1-4)

11. Also pray that:

> ... they will be caught when guilty
>
> ... they will desire the right kind of friends and be protected from the wrong kind
>
> ... that they will be kept from the wrong mate and saved for the right one
>
> ... that they will, along with those they wed, be kept pure until marriage.

Well, that should keep us busy for a while. Why not take one a day to pray for them. Remember, as you pray these things for your children, you are the model they are watching. Do they see you making good choices in how you spend your time, how you treat your mate, how you handle pressure and disappointments? These are all teaching times that God brings into your life for the purpose of learning and teaching Godly living. How are you doing?

Jeff, my son, was four-years-old. How I loved him and enjoyed his sweet personality and fun-loving spirit. He could turn any room into a party with a few toys and his incredible imagination. On this Friday, I had helped him clean up his toys and had put him in his room to play while I cleaned the house and raked, yes raked, the yellow shag carpet. You see, company was coming and I wanted the house to look perfect. (Actually, I wanted it to look like no one lived in it.) The cookies I made couldn't be touched, the carpet I raked couldn't be walked on, the book he wanted me to read couldn't be read and the tenderness of a mother's heart couldn't be shared because I had too much to do...for company. As I kept explaining this to Jeff, he looked up at me with those huge dark brown eyes and said, "Mommy, I wish I was company!"

"Ouch!" That hurt for a long time. As I reflected on that comment, I realized that my pride had gotten in the way of my motherhood. I was more concerned with looking "perfect" for company than with being "loving and available" to my son. I'm thankful that God used that lesson to teach me the importance of making right choices in small things.

I was more concerned with looking "perfect" for company than with being "loving and available" to my son.

Encouragement from God's Heart to Yours!

"And let us not lose heart in doing good, for in due time we shall reap if we do not grow weary."

(Galatians 6:9)

"…the effective prayer of a righteous man can accomplish much."

(James 5:16a)

"Little children, let us not love with word or with tongue, but in deed and truth."

(1 John 3:18)

"Humble yourselves, therefore, under the mighty hand of God, that He may exalt you at the proper time, casting all your anxiety upon Him because He cares for you."

(1 Peter 5:6-7)

Surrender from Your Heart to His!

Here I am again, Lord. Thanks for hearing me and being available to me. You know how frustrated I've been with some of the choices that my child has made. I've been so angry and hurt. Please help me to think of how you hurt when I make wrong choices. Help me to repent when I forget to trust my children to You, when I doubt your goodness and love for me, when I've wanted to give up on prayer because it doesn't seem to work. I ask you to renew my mind so that I will be able to support my children in prayer, teach them Your ways from a pure heart and bring joy to Your heart with my choices. I love you Father.

Your Child_____

Bible Study Questions for Chapter Four are on page 90.

Hope and Help for a Mother's Heart

Chapter Five

The Diversity of Motherhood

❦

*"Sometimes it seems a thankless job, at other times it's great.
And no two kids are quite alike, to each she must relate."*

*D*oes your home look more like a zoo than a family? Do you often wonder where one of your children came from? It's common to find many personalities in the same family and learning to accept them, relate to them and guide them definitely requires God's wisdom and patient understanding. Since moms are the ones that are home with the kids the most, this becomes one of our greatest challenges.

I've called the four basic personality types the perky, the passionate, the powerful and the pensive. The **perky personality** is fun-loving, people oriented, witty, optimistic and has lots of friends. This person loves to talk and talk and is good at motivating others. They also tend towards the following: they procrastinate, dislike details, are not goal oriented and they can easily control by charm. Some kids have the **powerful personality**, making them very goal oriented and outspoken. They are doers who love to solve problems. This type is a leader who is decisive and organized with a high energy level. The powerful also tends to be aggressive, control oriented and they easily climb over people to get what they want. The powerful don't like to be questioned, but obeyed.

Still others have a **passionate personality** and are sensitive, loyal, supporting and merciful. They are drawn to anyone who is hurting or needing encouragement. However, this type often has trouble saying no to anyone, and can be easily disappointed in others. You also might find the passionate parenting the parent. This personality can be inflexible and they don't handle disorder very well. The last type is the **pensive personality**. This child is more introverted and soft-spoken, but they actually read instructions and do things right. They are detail oriented and finish the job. This type of personality is not as outgoing and tends to avoid conflict and decision-making. They are also frustrated by disorder and don't understand people who aren't organized.

Can you see why your home often resembles a hassle rather than a haven? You're one person, with one personality, trying to discipline, train, mold and relate to all these various personality types. At times, it does seem impossible and we tend to do the following:

<u>We react rather than relate</u>. (Show frustration rather than train or speak in a way that they understand)

<u>We demand rather than disciple</u>. (Demand our way rather than build Godly character)

<u>We yell rather than yield</u>. (Respond before we listen to God's voice...telling us to deal calmly, lovingly with forbearance)

<u>We fight rather than fix</u>. (Get angry rather than seeking help from God's Word and prayer)

Are any of these reactions familiar to you? Are they hindering your ability to be a Godly mother? God didn't make a mistake, He placed that child in your family for a specific reason. He desires for you and your child to grow and mature together, understanding each other's differences. In fact, He doesn't just desire it, He requires it:

"And so, as those who have been chosen of God, holy and beloved, put on a heart of compassion, kindness, humility, gentleness and patience; bearing with one another and forgiving each other, whoever has a complaint against anyone; just as the Lord forgave you, so also should you."

(Colossians 3:12-13)

LET'S LOOK CAREFULLY AT GOD'S WORDS TO US AS MOTHERS:

Put on compassion – share in suffering, give aid and support, show mercy;

Put on kindness – be generous, warm-hearted, understanding;

Put on gentleness – be considerate or kind, not harsh;

Put on patience – have calm endurance, tolerant understanding, persevering;

Put on forbearance – have tolerance and restraint when provoked, accepting differences;

Put on forgiveness – to excuse for a fault, to pardon without resentment.

I know you're probably thinking that you don't see that this is written to mothers…right? Sorry, but I don't see anywhere in God's Word, and especially in this passage, that we are excused from these behaviors. It's just not there; and yet, we excuse our actions and reactions every day because we don't truly believe God understands. He not only understands, He orchestrates it. *"My purpose will be established, and I will accomplish all My good pleasure. Truly I have spoken; truly I will bring it to pass. I have planned it, surely I will do it."* (Isaiah 46:10b-11b)

As we seek to be obedient to God's word for our behavior each day, God will honor our obedience. (1 Corinthians 15:57-58) So what do we do with the differences in our children? <u>First, we stop trying to change the personality of our child. Instead, we seek God's direction in molding their character.</u> Secondly, we need to let each child know what God expects of them and then **we, as parents, train them in the way He created them, not as we wish they were.** Here are a few examples of how we can develop character in the lives of all personality types: (not a complete list)

1. Teach them fear (reverential respect) for the Lord. (Proverbs 19:23)
2. Teach them to control their tongue. (Proverbs 21:23)
3. Teach them that discipline is a part of being loved. (Proverbs 13:24)
4. Teach them that righteous living is more important than wealth. (Proverbs 16:8)
5. Teach them that rejecting knowledge (from parents, teachers) makes them a fool. (Proverbs 18:2)
6. Teach them the importance of humility. (Proverbs 27:1-2)
7. Teach them to be honest and ask forgiveness when wrong. (Proverbs 28:13)

We, as parents, train them in the way He created them, not as we wish they were.

The Diversity of Motherhood

Dear mom, I don't want this chapter to cause frustration or discouragement for you. Instead, I pray that you will be able to identify trouble spots and commit to change how you react or relate. I also pray that you can see the positive ways you can be training your children no matter what personality type they are.

As I've watched my latest granddaughter Lucy, learn to walk, I've noticed how each baby step is important. We cheer, we clap, we take pictures and our hearts rejoice with each new accomplishment. She may only take two steps but we're so proud. If she falls down, we quickly help her up and encourage her to try again. I was comparing this to how we treat our children later in life. Sometimes they only take two baby steps forward in their spiritual or emotional life, then they fall and we get upset rather than building them up and encouraging them to try again. Ephesians 4:29 warns us, "*Let no unwholesome word proceed from your mouth, but only such a word as is good for edification (building up), according to the need of the moment, that it may give grace to those who hear.*" (emphasis mine)

If you find yourself getting angry because of your child's differing personality or his faltering steps, ask for forgiveness from that child and from God and then make a fresh start. It's so important to remember that **our primary goal as parents is not to bring about perfection, but to faithfully seek to move them from where they are toward where God wants them to be.** This can't be done in our own strength, but by God's indwelling Spirit, Who will guide us moment by moment.

I'm so very grateful that my Heavenly Father is loving and patient with me in my faltering baby steps...aren't you?

Encouragement from God's Heart to Yours!

"Consider it a sheer gift, friends, when tests and challenges come at you from all sides. You know that under pressure, your faith-life is forced into the open and shows its true colors. So don't try to get out of anything prematurely. Let it do its work so you become mature and well-developed, not deficient in any way. If you don't know what you're doing, pray to the Father. He loves to help..."

(James 1:2-5) The Message

"The Lord is gracious and merciful; slow to anger and great in lovingkindness.... The Lord sustains all who fall, and raises up all who are bowed down.... The Lord is near to all who call upon Him, to all who call upon Him in truth. He will fulfill the desire of those who fear Him; He will also hear their cry and will save them."

(Psalm 145:8, 14, 18-19)

Surrender from Your Heart to His!

Dear Father:

I really need your help in relating to_____. You know how frustrated I've become and how tired I am. Forgive me for not seeing things clearly. Help me to realize that I can't change this child's personality but I can love_____with your love and seek to mold his/her character with your wisdom and guidance. Please Father, encourage my heart and help me make a fresh start today...for your glory! And thank you for always being there for me and for rejoicing in my baby steps. I love you, Father.

Your Child_____

Bible Study Questions for Chapter Five are on page 93.

Hope and Help for a Mother's Heart

Chapter Six

The Measure of Motherhood

"The task is overwhelming, bringing pain and also pleasure,
But what is done in Jesus' name is what the Lord will measure."

$\mathcal{S}$ ometimes we think a good mother is measured by the following list:

A good mother has the patience of Job with every child, every time.

A good mother has children who excel in academics and sports.

A good mother keeps all her family's clothes clean, mended, pressed and put away at all times.

A good mother appears instantly when any child yells "Mom!"

A good mother always prepares homemade, well-balanced, delicious meals.

A good mother never raises her voice.

A good mother is ready for company at a moment's notice.

A good mother does one craft every day with her children.

A good mother never needs to discipline her children in public.

A good mother never misses a practice, game or event of any kind.

A good mother keeps the house neat, looks terrific, keeps her body fit and has time to help at school and church.

Are we feeling sick yet? I definitely know the pressure of trying to be the perfect mother. When my children were small, my father was the pastor of our church of over 1500, my husband was an Elder in the church and the principal of the Christian School where our kids attended, and I was a Deaconess in the church. It was a triple whammy! Our poor children were being examined at every level, every day, and I felt tremendous pressure to make sure they were perfect and I was perfect. Guess what…it didn't work. The more I tried the more stress I put on all of us. **I was aiming at perfection rather than at pleasing my Lord.** When I realized that the root of this was pride, I had to confess how prideful I had become and how much I wanted people to see me, and my children, as "nearly perfect." I thought it was for God's glory, but truthfully, it was for my glory. (James 4:6-7)

I was aiming at perfection rather than at pleasing my Lord.

As I confessed my sin of pride and accepted God's forgiveness, He washed me with His comfort and gave me a new perspective on child-rearing. I began to see that my job was to "represent Jesus" in my daily life as a mother. To *"do all in the name of the Lord Jesus"* (Colossians 3:17a) was to do all as representing Jesus. This totally changed my outlook on mothering.

When my son or daughter disappointed me or disobeyed, I began asking myself, "How would Jesus handle this? What would be most important to Him right now? How can I show love and grace while disciplining them or training them?" Don't get me wrong, I certainly made lots of mistakes and pride crept in when I wasn't spiritually prepared, but my heart had changed and the Holy Spirit had fertile ground to work in.

May I just give you a simple example of this? When our children were small, we chose to take them into the worship service with us each Sunday, even though there were children's programs during the service that they could have attended. We wanted them to learn to sit quietly, respect God's House, get familiar with the great hymns of the faith, and learn the importance of worshiping together as a family. Our motives were right but sometimes my heart wasn't right. As Jeff or Jennifer would sometimes get fidgety or cause a small distraction, my heart would sink. Then, in my embarrassment, I would give them "the look that could kill" as my son calls it, and pour out my discipline later. My reaction didn't show concern for them but only proved that I was concerned about how I looked. When my heart changed, I brought things to help them sit through a long service, such as books or a pencil and paper. I relaxed when they acted normal and I began building them up for their efforts. If they faltered, it wasn't the end of the world anymore, but a part of their maturing process...and mine.

I thanked God for the work He had done in me when a lady who sat behind us commented that my child wasn't as quiet as usual and she really noticed it. Instead of being horrified, I smiled and said, "Aren't kids great, I love how God uses them to teach us patience and humility."

Are you wondering why I'm sharing all of this? Remember that this chapter is about the "Measure of Motherhood" and I want to give you some very good news. God doesn't measure us by how successful, smart, beautiful, well-behaved or popular our kids are. **He is looking to see how we represent Him in our training of them.** And He gives us the power and ability to do just that. We can't do it on our own. "*For it is God who is at work in you, both to will and to work for His good pleasure.*" (Philippians 2:13)

Just last week I spoke with a mother who was so discouraged. She shared how she had trained her son in the ways of the Lord, given Him all her love and godly counsel, taken him to church faithfully and now he had seemingly rejected it all. In her deep pain she cried, "It feels like it was all for nothing!" As my heart went out to her, I put my arm around her and shared that the training she had done for the Lord was not in vain. It was "in the bank" with the Lord, and no one could take it away. She didn't need to see how or when God was going to use it, she only needed to rest in the fact that she had been faithful to do her part and no one could rob that from her son. (Galatians 6:9) The rest was up to the Lord. When you're free from guilt and despair, you're free to move on and trust God with your child. That freedom allows you to grow in your love relationship with the Savior once again.

When you're free from guilt and despair, you're free to move on and trust God with your child.

Encouragement from God's Heart to Yours!

"To this end also we pray for you always that our God may count you worthy of your calling, and fulfill every desire for goodness and the work of faith with power; in order that the name of our Lord Jesus may be glorified in you, and you in Him, according to the grace of our God and the Lord Jesus Christ."

(2 Thessalonians 1:11-12)

"Suffer hardship with me, as a good soldier of Christ Jesus. No soldier in active service entangles himself in the affairs of everyday life, so that he may please the one who enlisted him as a soldier."

(2 Timothy 2:3-4)

"So don't get tired of doing what is good. Don't get discouraged and give up, for we will reap a harvest of blessing at the appropriate time."

(Galatians 6:9, NLT)

Hope and Help for a Mother's Heart
Surrender from Your Heart to His!

Dear Father:

Thank you for freeing me from the tyranny of trying to be perfect. I'm sorry that I've let my pride get in the way of what You wanted me to do. Please change my focus as I rely on you each day to renew my mind. Even when I'm terribly disappointed in my child, please help me represent You in a way that truly pleases You. May I be more concerned with what You think than with what others think. And Father, please do your work in my child as I leave_____in your capable, loving hands.

Your Child_____

Bible Study Questions for Chapter Six are on page 96.

Chapter Seven

The Love of Motherhood

❧

"So let the love of Jesus flow freely out through you.
And love them just the way they are and not for what they do."

D o you know that feeling of being so angry and frustrated with a child that no love is coming through? You can hardly look her in the eye, let alone speak lovingly to her. And yet, God's Word says we are to *"speak the truth in love"* (Ephesians 4:15a) and the *"answer of the tongue"* should be from the Lord. (Proverbs 16:1) So what should we do about this when the love isn't flowing and our heart feels dry as a bone? Personally, I have to take my anger to the Lord. I tell Him the details of my situation, then wait on Him to calm me down and clear my thinking.

You see, when you're hurt or angry, your perspective is distorted by your emotions. You cannot think clearly and let God's love flow freely through you, until your emotions and your hurts are given over to the Lord. When you give a reaction based on your emotions, it often makes the situation worse as it makes the child more angry or distant.

Let me give you a visual picture. I want you to picture a beautiful ceramic pitcher that has been filled with mud. It doesn't really matter how beautiful the pitcher is if mud is all that comes out of it. So, you decide to change the contents; you pour out a little of the mud and add some delicious sweet lemonade. Then you begin to pour again. What do you have…watered down mud. So you pour half of the mud out and fill the other half with lemonade. Does the sweetness of the lemonade come through now or is it still a dirty, muddy mixture? Of course, you know that it is. You see, the lemonade will always be tainted by the mud, even if there's only a very small portion in the pitcher. It will make the lemonade distasteful.

To make the contents of the pitcher usable and refreshing, you have to totally empty the mud out and thoroughly wash it. Then you can refill it with lemonade and enjoy it. David prayed, *"Create in me a clean heart, O God, and renew a steadfast spirit within me. Restore to me the joy of Thy salvation, and sustain me with a willing spirit."* (Psalm 51:10, 12)

To love our children just as they are, we need for God to create a clean heart in us. We must confess the sin of acting apart from His will. We cannot bring about a clean heart on our own, but God can and will as we give up the muddy waters of our lives. Then, as we refill our thoughts with the truths of His Word, He will "sustain us with a willing spirit." Only then can we look at the thirteenth chapter of I Corinthians and be ready to have His love flow freely out through us to our children.

1 CORINTHIANS 13, "THE LOVE CHAPTER"
A MOTHER'S PARAPHRASE

If I keep the house beautifully and dress my children in the latest fashions, but do not deeply love each one, as God created him or her, my efforts will be worthless.

The Love of Motherhood

If I have read all the books on discipline and faithfully attend Bible study, but do not lovingly put what I have learned into practice, it will be worthless.

If I give of my time generously to help others, to work at church and school and do not do it out of a heart of love, it is to no avail.

Love is patient when my children make mistakes or disappoint me time after time.

Love is being kind to my children and husband even when I've had a rough day and don't feel like it.

Love isn't jealous of others who have nicer clothes, a better house or more well-behaved children. Love is being genuinely happy for them.

Love doesn't embarrass those I love by being selfish or demanding.

Love doesn't nag and does not seek to get even when I've been hurt.

Love means I never give up on my children's and husband's ability to change and grow in the Lord. Nor do I hold it against them if they are not growing as I feel they should.

Love endures anything while still maintaining a constant love for the one involved.

Love is not being depressed about the present or future but remembering there's always hope in the Lord.

No matter what I do for my family or how well I think I'm doing as a mother, if I don't allow God to love others through me, I am missing the most important aspects of motherhood.

C. Hopson

There's another important aspect of love that I must bring up at this point, and that is discipline. You might think it's strange to bring this up in the chapter about love, but listen to God's words:

"My child, don't ignore it when the Lord disciplines you, and don't be discouraged when He corrects you. For the Lord disciplines those He loves, and He punishes those he accepts as His children. As you endure this divine discipline, remember that God is treating you as His own children. Whoever heard of a child who was never disciplined? If God doesn't discipline you as He does all of His children, it means that you are illegitimate and are not really His children after all."

(Hebrews 12:5-8, New Living Translation)

Do you see how important Biblical discipline is? It proves that we are loved by God, and it also proves that we love our children. When our children were very young, we lived in a neighborhood where the kids played together in the front yard almost every day. The moms would gather on the front lawn with a cup of coffee and chat while watching the children play their games. Our next-door neighbors had four children who were well provided for in the material sense, but not in the emotional or spiritual sense. Their mother was there for them but she never disciplined them for talking back, bad attitudes or direct disobedience. I would often take one of my children aside to remind them about something or take them inside to be disciplined for disobedience.

One day, while sitting comfortably with my kids on the lawn, five-year-old Mary threw a temper tantrum right in front of all of us. Her mother simply lit up another cigarette, shook her head and went on with her conversation. After they had returned home for their lunch, my young son said, "Mommy, I don't think Mary's mom loves her." I was quite startled by the statement and asked him why he thought that. He quickly answered, "Because she doesn't spank her when she's doing bad things." I took Jeff in my arms and hugged him and thanked God that the message was getting through that love and discipline go hand in hand.

In loving your children as God would have you love them, are you being obedient in the area of discipline? To help you with this, here are the five steps for effective discipline for all ages:

INSTRUCTION

We must teach them right and wrong at each age. When they're toddlers, we need to teach them what they can and can't touch and when they can throw something (a ball) and when they can't (food). With teenagers, they need to be taught what you expect of them in the area of respect, purity, homework, dating etc. The teaching changes with each age level but the instruction must be given. When my children decided that the grocery store was a safe place to fuss for things, pout, or whine because they were tired, I realized that I had neglected their instruction. **Their behavior was my fault, not theirs.** The next time we went, we sat in the car before entering the store and I explained to them what behavior I expected in the store and what the consequences of their disobedience would be. Then I moved on to the next phase of discipline, which is reinforcement.

REINFORCEMENT

Reinforcement is so necessary to make sure your child was listening when you gave instructions. If necessary, remind them of your previous instruction and have them repeat it back to you. Then you ask them to repeat what the consequences will be if they disobey. This simple step will solve many problems if you will remember to do it. When my kids were teenagers and began dating, my husband and I would ask them to repeat what we expected of them on a date. We would ask when they were supposed to be home (11:00 pm, even in college) and what the consequences would be of a late arrival. If a child at any age goes against the direct instruction you have given, correction must follow! (Toddlers: Don't get out of bed again or I will have to give you a spanking. Elementary school: You must finish your homework and clean up your room or you won't be able to go to the party.)

One of the biggest mistakes Christian parents make is not following through with the appropriate discipline for their child's actions.

CONSEQUENCES

This is where the consequence for the action takes place. In over thirty-five years of counseling families and being involved in children's lives through Christian Education, I have witnessed the devastating results of children being raised without consequences. One of the biggest mistakes Christian parents make is not following through with the appropriate discipline for their child's actions. This leads to bullies, to me-centered living, to poor work ethics, to disrespect of parents and authorities and, ultimately, to walking away from God. Because the child didn't see consequences for their wrong choices, they didn't learn that there would be consequences for wrong spiritual choices. How I wish I could somehow implant this truth in the heart of every parent when their children are born.

Here is what God says about this: "No discipline is enjoyable while it is happening, it is painful! But afterward there will be a quiet harvest of right living for those who are trained in this way." (Hebrews 12:11) It's very important to notice that proper discipline is painful. Whether it's a spanking or a privilege taken away, it must cause real sorrow and pain or it will not produce the end result that is promised. Again, we must look carefully at this verse and see that the harvest of right living or righteousness comes to those who are "trained" by discipline. Training means that it is used consistently, it is practiced over and over. Therefore, we as parents must faithfully, consistently give consequences for wrong choices so that our children will reap a life of right choices that honor God. Here is a pattern that my husband and I followed with our children when they chose to disobey.

TRAINING CHILDREN TO OBEY (FOR ALL AGES)

1. Ask your child, "What did I tell you?"

2. Ask your child, "What did you do?" (Don't go any farther until your child is willing to admit this!)

3. Ask your child "Did you choose to obey or disobey?" (Always wait for them to say what they chose to do.)

4. Say, "Because you chose to disobey, and because I love you so much, I need to help you remember to obey next time." (This is so important for all ages!)

5. Give proper discipline for age and situation. (Always calmly, never in anger.)

6. Have the child ask for forgiveness from you and any others who have been affected. (As their heart is ready, they learn to ask forgiveness from God at this stage too.)

7. Always pray with the child and restore the relationship.

RESTITUTION

At this stage in the discipling process, we must help the child right the wrong. It may involve saying they are sorry to you and to their brother or sister. (Make sure the heart attitude shows repentance or the disciplinary action may need to be repeated or extended.) Maybe they need to return something that didn't belong to them or they need to apologize to a teacher or admit that they cheated. If something happened at a friend's house, have your child call and apologize to the parents and to the friend. This aspect is difficult for the child and the parent but is absolutely necessary to deter them from wanting to repeat the wrong.

REASSURANCE

When the four stages have been gone through properly, you are ready to reassure your child of your love for them. Never reject a child after discipline and always make sure that the parent who disciplined the child is the one who reaffirms, hugs and encourages him or her. If the child doesn't want this from you, the heart isn't surrendered yet and the process has not been completed. If this occurs, you might tell your child to spend some time in his or her room until the heart is changed and they are ready to restore fellowship with you. Depending on the age, you might have them read scriptures or you may want to spend extra time praying and talking with them about what is still troubling them.

As I conclude this chapter let me share what Gary Smalley, a renowned author, counselor and founder of Today's Family, says in his book "The Key to Your Child's Heart." "I have concluded that the two most important factors in raising children are:

(1) establishing clearly defined and understood rules in the home; limits that the children know they cannot violate without consequence.

(2) a commitment to love each child in a warm, affectionate and supportive way."

Encouragement from God's Heart to Yours!

"To discipline and reprimand a child produces wisdom, but a mother is disgraced by an undisciplined child."

(Proverbs 29:15, NLT)

"If you refuse to discipline your children, it proves you don't love them; if you love your children, you will be prompt to discipline them.

(Proverbs 13:24, NLT)

"And everyone who hears these words of Mine, and does not act upon them, will be like a foolish man, who built his house upon the sand. And the rain descended, and the floods came, and the winds blew, and burst against that house; and it fell, and great was its fall."

(Matthew 7:26-27)

"Do not fear for I am with you; do not anxiously look about you, for I am your God. I will strengthen you, surely I will help you, surely I will uphold you with My righteous right hand."

(Isaiah 41:10)

Surrender from Your Heart to His!

Dear Father:

Sometimes I feel so inadequate to be a mother. I fail at loving and I fail at consistent discipline. But Father, you know my heart and you know that I desire to be all that You want me to be. Please forgive me for my mistakes and give me your strength to be faithful just one day at a time. Please free me from fear and worry and keep me focused on trusting You to help me through each day. I love you Father.

Your Child_____

Bible Study Questions for Chapter Seven are on page 99.

Chapter Eight

The God of Motherhood

❧

"For that's the way our Father loves, how thankful we should be,
That His love isn't measured by the good or bad He sees."

Dear Carol:

I'm sorry but I just can't love you anymore. You've just disappointed me too many times. I've poured out my love on you for so long but you've made so many wrong choices. Remember when your husband lost his job and you got so anxious and couldn't sleep? And then there was that time that your friend betrayed you and you held that bitterness in your heart for way too long. I just can't forget how many times you let me down when I wanted you to trust Me. I just don't know how to reach you anymore so I'm giving up on you. Please don't call on me again!

Wouldn't it be horrible if God really treated us that way? Fortunately, that will never happen, and that fact alone should make us rejoice every moment of our lives. If God loved us according to our successes or failures, it would be hopeless. Yet, that is often how we love our children. In this chapter I want to focus on God's unconditional love for us so that we will know what it feels like and be able to pass it on to those God has given us to love. There's no way that I can cover God's love for His children in this chapter or in a whole volume of books. So, as I prayed about this, I sat quietly before the Lord and reflected on what aspects of God's love have been so comforting to me as a mother and a wife. I'll simply share those four for your comfort and encouragement.

GOD ACCEPTS ME AS I AM!

Have you ever been afraid that someday, someone would figure out that you weren't really what you seem to be? If only they really knew your thoughts and failures, surely you'd never be loved again. Especially if they saw how you responded to your kids a few times. And what about your mate? How much would he love you if he really knew what you thought of him sometimes? It would not be a pretty picture. But God's love is different! He loves us just as we are, knowing every thought, every fault, every failure and doubt. That's love so amazing!

GOD FORGIVES ME…ALWAYS!

Okay, I have a hard time forgiving someone after they've hurt me or lied to me three times. You know how it is when that special child God gave you says, "I'm sorry, I forgot" for the hundredth time. Do you really believe him and accept the apology or is there a seed of unbelief and resentment? But God says, "If we confess our sins to Him, He is faithful and just to forgive us and to cleanse us from every wrong." (1 John 1:9, NLT) How many times does God say He will forgive us…ten…fifty…a hundred? No number is mentioned and there is no limit to His forgiveness of His child.

I'm reminded of a story that my dad told me. While walking out to his mailbox one day, he spotted a very small toddler out in the middle of the busy road. There were no adults in sight and the road was dangerous, so my dad hurried out his driveway to bring the young child to safety. When he got close to him, he realized that he was filthy dirty and his diapers were definitely full. He grabbed his little hand and quickly led him to the safety of the sidewalk. He then squatted down on his level and comforted him while watching for any frantic mother in the vicinity. Now, my dad loves babies and toddlers more than almost anyone I know, but he decided not to pick him up, partly because of the filth and smell. As he soothed him and talked to him he spotted a car driving hastily by, then screech to a halt and back up. The panicked woman left the car running in the middle of the road, jumped out and ran over to her son. Without the slightest hesitation, she swept up that smelly, messy toddler in her arms and smothered him with kisses and hugs. She almost forgot to thank my father for finding him in her total relief and joy at finding her son.

Don't you suppose that's how our Heavenly Father feels when we come to Him with our ugly sins? I can just see Him enfolding me, with my sinful dirty rags, in His loving arms. And then, as I confess my sins to Him, His righteousness changes my clothes from filthy to fit for the King. That's love so amazing!

God Knows My Heart!

I really hate to be misunderstood. It hurts me deeply when I intend to do something kind or helpful and someone misunderstands or rejects the act and me. I'm reminded of a very hurtful time in my life. A suicidal young mother came to me for friendship and counsel. I spent hours, days, weeks and months praying with her, talking her through her fears in the night hours and providing a place of safety in my own home whenever she dropped by. In the end, she turned her anger on me and spread rumors about me and rejected my friendship totally. It was terribly painful, as I had given so much time and love to try to help her and I didn't find out the reason for her rejection until years later. (It had nothing to do with me and everything to do with her husband's adultery.) However, the pain lasted for a long time.

My comfort and peace came when I finally realized, and truly believed, that God knew my heart.

But God's love is different. My comfort and peace came when I finally realized, and truly believed, that God knew my heart. (Psalm 139:1-6) He was the judge that mattered and I could trust Him! But, did I care more about what He knew about me or what others thought about me? Because of my love for God, I had to give up my precious "reputation" and trust Him with my "character." As I released my anger and bitterness to Him, He comforted me with these words:

"This suffering is all part of what God has called you to. Christ, who suffered for you, is your example. Follow in His steps. He never sinned and He never deceived anyone. He did not retaliate when He was insulted. When He suffered, He did not threaten to get even. He left His case in the hands of God, who always judges fairly."

(1 Peter 2:21-23, NLT)

God doesn't listen to Satan's accusations about me or you. He, your Righteous Judge, knows you. He knows the truth about the thoughts and intents of your heart. Of course, there are times when your desires have been selfish and wrong and He deals with those. But, He also knows your heart's desire as a mother and He will keep His word to you. Barbara Johnson, author of "Fresh Elastic for Stretched Out Moms" says, "God gives the final score on a life when the game is over. The game is not over with your children yet! God didn't promise we'd be leading at the half, but only that we would win the game!" "But thanks be to God, who gives us the victory through our Lord Jesus Christ." (2 Corinthians 15:57) That's love so amazing!

GOD DOES WHAT'S BEST FOR ME!

Do you feel like God is always doing what is best for you? If you're honest, you'll say that it certainly doesn't seem like He does. But let's again go to the truth of God's Word.

"What man among you, when his son shall ask him for a loaf, will give him a stone? Or if he shall ask for a fish, he will not give him a snake, will he? If you then, being evil, know how to give good gifts to your children, how much more shall your Father Who is in heaven give what is good to those who ask Him!"

(Matthew 7:9-11)

To try to understand this, let me tell you one more story about my grandchild. Lucy Marie was barely ten months old and was crawling around the family room pulling herself up on everything. I was in the adjoining kitchen, preparing supper for the family who were playing outside. Lucy was standing by the sofa and I turned to take something out of my lower oven and place it on the counter. As I turned around to close the 400 degree oven door, I saw Lucy reaching up for that same door. She often played with the dishwasher door when it was open and this was about the same level for her. In my panic, I reached over and knocked her away from that fiery door as quickly and forcefully as I could. Lucy fell down on her bottom and her lip quivered and the tears began to come. Then, my beloved granddaughter, whom I had showered so much love on, who literally lit up when she saw me, who knew that I would do anything to make her smile, gave me a look of total disbelief. It was as if she was saying, "How could you, Nana? I thought you loved me!"

As I picked her up in my arms and comforted her through my own tears, I realized that there was no way to explain my actions to a 10-month-old. She was not capable of understanding what I had done and couldn't realize that it was for her good, out of my deep love for her. She only felt the rejection and pain of it. Let me ask you a question. Did I do it because I wanted to be mean to her, to cause her pain, or was it because I loved her so much? You know the answer. Later that day, the Lord so lovingly showed me that this was how He feels sometimes. He has to do things for our good, for our growth, out of His love for us, but we are too immature to understand it. And so, we just have to believe His words to us and trust that He loves us and wants what is best for us...even when it deeply hurts Him. That's love so amazing!

Encouragement from God's Heart to Yours!

"...I have loved you with an everlasting love; therefore I have drawn you with lovingkindness."

(Jeremiah 31:3b)

"And I am convinced that nothing can ever separate us from His love. Death can't, and life can't. The angels can't, and the demons can't. Our fears for today, our worries about tomorrow, and even the powers of hell can't keep God's love away. Whether we are high above the sky or in the deepest ocean, nothing in all creation will ever be able to separate us from the love of God that is revealed in Christ Jesus our Lord."

(Romans 8:38-39, NLT)

"This is real love. It is not that we loved God, but that He loved us and sent His Son as a sacrifice to take away our sins."

(1 John 4:10, NLT)

SURRENDER FROM YOUR HEART TO HIS!

Dear Father:

I admit that I don't understand your love sometimes. It's so easy to get my eyes off of what You did for me at the cross, and focus on how I feel. Please forgive me for doubting you, and I ask You to walk me through these next few days and weeks as I learn to trust your love for me once again. Help me to not rely on my emotions but on truth. Help me to keep your Word in my heart so that I will not sin against you by my doubts. And, thank you for your amazing love, dear Father. I'm so very grateful that it isn't based on my perfection, but on Your promise.

Your Child_____

Bible Study Questions for Chapter Eight are on page 102.

Chapter Nine

The Attitude of Motherhood

❧

*"So as you go about your day, throw expectations out.
Give up those disappointments, that make you want to pout."*

Wouldn't you love to have a sign on your front door that read "No Pouting Allowed!" (Especially for your children.) But guess what? That would mean you too, mom! Doesn't it feel good to pout…at least for a little while? Why is that; why does it come so easily to some of us? I think it's because we have such high expectations in our everyday lives. I know we've had a chapter on broken dreams and sacrifices, but this one is about those little things that trip us up over and over. It's those times when we know we need an attitude adjustment, quickly.

I used to have such grandiose expectations of what Christmas or Thanksgiving dinner would be like at my house. Yes, even as a grandmother this has still crept into my life at times. I'd plan for days and weeks how it would be and I'd set the huge dining room table with beautiful decorations, my best china, small favors for each family member and even place cards. It was a labor of love and I had all the expectations of a long, lazy meal, with everyone enjoying the food, the family and the decorations I had so lovingly created. The picture in my mind was nearly perfect and would be a beautiful memory for years to come.

Now, let's match the reality of one Thanksgiving to my expectations for that day. After laboring many hours over the delicious turkey dinner and all the fixings, I called everyone to the table. About four out of thirteen came at first, making it difficult to know how to keep the food hot, which was already lovingly placed on the table. As I kept calling, one child had to go to the bathroom, one had to be disciplined for an attitude problem, one got cranky and was put down for a nap, leaving several open spaces at the table. Next, an adult got up to help the child who was stuck in the bathroom, one had to leave the table again to see if the disciplined child was ready to come out, another's business beeper went off and so he left to answer it and so on. I think you get the picture. I sat at one end of the table, with a bewildered look, staring helplessly at my husband. My "labor of love" dinner was getting cold, no one was noticing the decorations and my stress level was on the rise. There was not one time that the entire family was at the table together that day. Do you identify with any of this? Your situation might be very different, but if you'll admit it, you have expectations that aren't being met either.

My "labor of love" dinner was getting cold, no one was noticing the decorations and my stress level was on the rise.

When the Lord moved my husband and me several states away from our children and grandchildren, I had a different view of holiday dinners. We spent several major holidays with no family at all with us. And, as I would reflect on past family gatherings, my heart would be warmed at all the fun times, the twists and turns of the day, and the hilarious memories of some of those dinners. Now, it would have been wonderful to just have family in my house...anywhere...doing anything! It just wasn't that important to have a perfect meal anymore. What was important was just being together.

Let's take a look at some of our most ridiculous expectations.

- We expect the house to stay clean after we've cleaned it.
- We expect the family to notice and comment on how nice everything looks.
- We expect our kids to appreciate the time we spend in the car bussing them to all their activities.
- We expect our in-laws to love us and think we are the best thing that ever happened to their son.
- We expect a giant hug of gratitude for the clean clothes that have miraculously reappeared in their drawers.
- We expect that what's important to us will also be important to our husbands and kids.
- We expect our kids to appreciate and accept our advice because we're their mother.
- We expect that Christmas will be perfect...this year.
- We expect that everyone will enjoy and appreciate the meal we've just prepared after a very long day.
- We expect to have peace in the bathroom.
- We expect that someday, every family member will wake up and realize what fantastic mothers we really are.

I know you have great expectations and it's so hard to let them go and accept things as they really are. But when you learn that the only One who can handle our expectations is the Lord, it will free you to enjoy the moment and find humor in the upset plans. One way to do this is to send up "telegraph prayers," as Amy Carmichael calls them. It's just a quick cry for help, such as, "Patience now, Lord" or "Please help, Lord." As human beings, we all live with the need to be loved, supported, understood, respected, encouraged and treasured. Is that really too much to ask? Not if you ask it from the right One! Now let's take a look at what we can really expect from our wonderful Lord in any circumstance.

- We can expect changes in our plans, but God's immediate help to deal with it.

- We can expect to be disappointed in our children, but God will never disappoint us.

- We can expect to grow and mature in whatever God allows to happen in our lives. (If we choose to trust Him.)

- We can expect to live without guilt and regrets as we leave our expectations in His hands.

- We can expect to have great opportunities to put God's love and grace on display in our lives.

- We can expect to be forgiven every time we fall.

- We can expect a lot more joy in our lives because we've let go of our impossible expectations.

- We can expect great peace as we accept God's rearrangement of our days.

- We can expect a great future reward for endurance, patience and perseverance.

- We can expect to be loved, supported, understood, respected, encouraged and treasured by our Heavenly Father.

I'm feeling so much better already, aren't you?

Encouragement from God's Heart to Yours!

"Above all else, guard your heart, for it affects everything you do."

(Proverbs 4:23, NLT)

"No soldier in active service entangles himself in the affairs of everyday life, so that he may please the one who enlisted him."

(2 Timothy 2:4)

"I have fought the good fight, I have finished the course, I have kept the faith; in the future there is laid up for me the crown of righteousness, which the Lord, the righteous Judge, will award to me on that day..."

(2 Timothy 4:7-8)

SURRENDER FROM MY HEART TO HIS!

Dear Father:

I think I've been guilty of pouting lately and I'd like to ask you to forgive me. I know I have so much to be thankful for but I seem to easily get my eyes on the wrong things. Please help me let go of my unreal expectations. Help me to make my family feel more loved and accepted just as they are, and help me to not miss the joy of the moments I have with them. I know that there's a lot I need to teach my children, but please help me allow them to be imperfect and human. Father, I want to do what's right so please guard my heart from anger or bitterness. Thank you that I can always count on You to meet my needs. I love you Father.

Your Child_____

Bible Study Questions for Chapter Nine are on page 105.

Chapter Ten

The Grace of Motherhood

❧

*"So thank God for His blessings, His mercy and His grace,
Then let Him fill your life with joy, as each new day you face."*

How do I even begin to write about grace, God's amazing grace? I've read such remarkable books on grace that I feel totally inadequate to even begin this chapter. And yet, the poem that God gave me, which begins each chapter in this book, ends with grace. And I know that I'm supposed to write about it at this point. It's late at night and God just hasn't released me from writing today and so, I'll continue to share what He gives me. You see, each book that I have written has been done out of obedience to my Lord. I never intended to write a book, but as I'm finishing my fifth book, I look back and see that it was only God's grace that enabled me to do it. By His grace, the words, illustrations and scriptures came to me, and by His grace so many lives have been ministered to.

Grace, to me, is two-part. First of all, there's saving grace, which I received when I accepted Jesus Christ as my Lord and Savior. This aspect of grace forgave me from past, present and future sin and clothed me in His righteousness, making me acceptable in God's sight and fit to spend eternity with Him.

(Ephesians 2:8-9) The other aspect of grace is God's enabling grace. It is God enabling His servants to do what they could not otherwise do. In the Old Testament, we read that Noah found grace, and Esther found grace and Daniel found grace. It seems that they were all given God's grace, to do extraordinary things for God's glory. I think mothering is one of the most difficult and yet, most extraordinary opportunities a woman ever has, to do something remarkable, for God's glory. But it often seems too overwhelming, and maybe even impossible in our own strength.

I think mothering is one of the most difficult and yet, most extraordinary opportunities a woman ever has, to do something remarkable, for God's glory.

I know that you have days, maybe weeks and months, where you feel so inadequate to the task. You wonder how your children will ever grow up to be responsible, mature, loving adults. You wonder if that wayward child will ever return to the Lord or maybe you can't imagine how you'll ever be able to open your child's closed spirit. At these times, you are gripped by worry and fear, which paralyzes you emotionally. That's because the Greek word for worry comes from two words, literally meaning to divide the mind. A worrier has a divided mind. (Philippians 4:6; Mark 4:19) A divided mind keeps you from trusting the Lord, keeps you from believing in miracles and keeps you from being the mother God intends for you to be. (Luke 8:14)

A few months ago, I was thinking about whether or not I would write a fifth book. People kept asking me if I was writing another one. The task seemed so overwhelming to me, nearly impossible. It's not something I would choose to do. I'm a people person and I love being out meeting with people, sharing God's truths with them or encouraging them through their difficult times. And yet, God kept nudging me to write again, and so I began to think about how each book has been accomplished. To look at the possibility of writing a whole book, from beginning to end, editing it, choosing a cover and getting it published, doesn't even seem plausible to me. But, I remember how the Lord first told me to just sit down and write, one sentence at a time, one day at a time. I couldn't get caught up in the whole picture, just write what God gave me that day and trust Him for the rest. It was simply a moment by moment acceptance of His grace. Five books later I look back and can't even see how it all got done, but my heart is flooded with gratitude to the Lord for seeing me through it all.

The important thing is to...just do the little things today in obedience to the Lord.

I think that mothering is a lot like writing a book. To look at all the responsibilities, the work, the beginning and the end, the finished product you desire, is just too overwhelming. The important thing is to...

just do the little things today in obedience to the Lord...
keep a sweet spirit when it's difficult...
look for small blessings...
use daily annoyances to teach eternal truths...
forgive and forget quickly...
love unconditionally...
accept changes you didn't plan on...
be consistent.

Then one day, maybe twenty years later, you'll look back and see all God did to see you and your precious children through, even in your weakness. Too tough? Not with God's grace!

"And God is able to make all grace abound to you, that always having all sufficiency in everything, you may have an abundance for every good deed."

(2 Corinthians 9:8)

He's there with you every moment of every day, to pour His riches into your life. He is able…are you willing?

If you're still wondering why you're not experiencing that amazing grace He offers, maybe you need to hear about the "mailbox principle." At times in my life, I have not been able to trust God's grace and I used to wonder what I was doing wrong. Was I not strong enough? Was I not spiritual enough? What was my problem? Then God, in His loving way, gave me the answer through a simple mailbox.

Picture this: You've just written a letter to your best friend, inviting her to go on a trip with you. You explain that the expenses are all paid but she needs to let you know right away so that you can get the tickets and make plans. You address, seal and stamp the envelope and take it to the mailbox, that big blue one on the corner. As you get there, you pull down the handle with your left hand revealing the opening, and with your right hand you put almost all of the letter into the mailbox.

At this point, 99% of the letter is inside of the mailbox and so you close that little door, holding on to only the tiniest corner of the envelope. Then you stand there and wait…and wait…and wait. You begin to get very frustrated because you're not receiving an answer and you really need to know. You explained all the details, you said how urgent it was that she mail you an answer and yet the answer doesn't come. You start thinking that she's not much of a friend because she doesn't even care enough to write back.

Now let me ask you a simple question. Why didn't you get an answer? Was it because she didn't care or because she didn't value your friendship? No, it was because you never mailed it...you never did let go! Experiencing God's grace, as a mother, is simply letting go.

ON LETTING GO!

Dear Lord, I just don't understand
What's happened in my life.
Things weren't supposed to go this way
And cause me so much strife.

I've come to You so many times
And prayed so very much.
But nothing seems to work, dear Lord,
I feel so out of touch.

The worries just won't go away
And fear consumes my heart.
I think that things just might get worse
Why don't You do your part?

Dear child, please listen to my voice,
There's something you should know.
I want so much to lift your load,
But first, you must let go!

C. Hopson

Are you ready to mail that problem right now? Will you let go of all your fears and frustrations regarding your children? Can you see what corner you're still hanging on to? When you can identify that, ask God's forgiveness and then release everything into the mailbox of His love. It's such a safe place to be and He always answers His mail.

"Keep on asking, and you will be given what you ask for. Keep on looking, and you will find. Keep on knocking, and the door will be opened. For everyone who asks, receives. Everyone who seeks, finds. And the door is opened to everyone who knocks. You parents, if your children ask for a loaf of bread, do you give them a stone instead? Or if they ask for a fish, do you give them a snake? Of course not! If you sinful people know how to give good gifts to your children, how much more will your heavenly father give good gifts to those who ask Him."

(Matthew 7:7-11, NLT)

Go on! Mail it today!

Encouragement from God's Heart to Yours!

"Beloved, let us love one another, for love is from God; and everyone who loves is born of God and knows God. The one who does not love does not know God, for God is love."

(1 John 4:7-8)

"There is no fear in love; but perfect love casts out fear, because fear involves punishment, and one who fears is not perfected in love. We love because He first loved us."

(1 John 4:18-19)

"See how great a love the Father has bestowed upon us, that we should be called children of God; and such we are..."

(1 John 3:1a)

Surrender from My Heart to His!

Dear Father:

Thank you for your amazing grace! I'm so sorry that I take it for granted so often and even forget about it. Yet, there have been many times in my life when your grace is the only thing that got me through. Sometimes, it's been so difficult for me to understand your love and I realize that I don't need to always understand it, but just trust You. Please help me let go of_____ and give you complete control. Forgive me for hanging on for so long. Thank you for loving me, forgiving me and enabling me, by your grace, to be the mother you want me to be. I love you Father.

Your Child_____

Bible Study Questions for Chapter Ten are on page 108.

"My Daughter, From Lace to Grace"

It begins with her face,
That delicate chin, her rosebud nose
And toothless grin.

She moves to pink lace,
From bonnet to toes, caressing her frame
With ribbons and bows.

We're then into place,
The places she finds, to stash all her toys
And make lipstick designs.

And then she's an ace,
At making mud pies, and weed-filled bouquets
Bringing tears to my eyes.

From lace to an ace, how time has flown,
And my precious daughter has certainly grown!

From here you must trace,
Her pathway is clear, just follow the phone cord
Attached to her ear.

And then it's a race,
From morning 'til dusk, to get her to things
She feels are a must!

She's also a case,
Of emotions and fears, up-days and down-days
Mixed up with tears.

Hope and Help for a Mother's Heart

The next stage is space,
She's pulling away, making new choices
Day after day.

From lace to space, how time has flown,
And my beautiful daughter has certainly grown!

The last stage is grace,
The grace that I see, as she is full grown,
And returns to me.

Now a mother and wife
She's brought so much joy, I hardly remember
How she could annoy.

And I see all along
That God's grace was near, helping us both
To mature through the years.

From lace into grace, what a wonderful end,
For my daughter is now, my very best friend.

Carol Hopson

A Note from the Author

As you've read through these pages, beginning with a mother's sacrifices and ending with God's grace for mothers, I pray that you have truly found peace, hope and joy...

As you let go of...

Your child...

Your dreams...

Your failures...

And your plans.

May you be ready to grab hold of...

His power...

His love...

His forgiveness...

And His grace.

And, may you truly trust the Savior...

To listen to you attentively...

To love you unconditionally...

To work in you miraculously

and

Give you hope abundantly.

"This hope we have as an anchor of the soul, a hope both sure and steadfast..."

(Hebrews 6:19a)

INTRODUCTION TO THE BIBLE STUDY

These Bible study questions are written for group or individual study. They are written for the following purpose:

- To encourage you if you're weary or discouraged
- To give you hope where you feel there is none
- To give you God's principles for child-rearing
- To help you seriously evaluate your relationship with your children and with your Lord
- To help you understand God's purpose for you in your role as mother and as God's child, through studying God's Word
- To remind you of God's incredible love for you, His precious child

"Thy word I have treasured in my heart, that I may not sin against Thee."

"Teach me good discernment and knowledge, for I believe in Thy commandments."

"Thy testimonies are wonderful; therefore my soul observes them. The unfolding of Thy words gives light; it gives understanding to the simple."
(Psalm 119:11, 66, 129, 130)

Study Questions for Chapter One

1. What do you feel you are sacrificing as a mother right now?

2. Is that difficult for you? Why or why not?

3. Read Psalm 139:1-6 in several translations and answer the following:

   a. How much does God know about you? (Be specific)

   b. What comfort does that give you as a mother?

c. What is the importance of Him going before you and behind you as a mother?

4. How have your eyes turned inward lately and what has been the result?

5. According to these verses, what can you do to change your daily perspective?

   a. Psalm 34:1

   b. Psalm 34:13-14

   c. Psalm 55:22

d. Psalm 37:30-31

e. Psalm 61:5-8

f. Proverbs 3:5-6

6. Is there something or someone that you need to "sacrifice" to the Lord right now?

STUDY QUESTIONS FOR CHAPTER TWO

1. How would you rate your prayer life right now?

2. If you rated yourself poor or needs improvement, why do you think that is? (no time to pray, not sure how to pray, not sure it works etc.)

3. What circumstance comes to the front of your mind right now, that causes you to be greatly shaken? (Read Psalm 16:8)

How does focusing on this circumstance affect...
You:

Your marriage:

Your children:

4. What promises and truths from God's Word can you " set before you" so that you will not be shaken next time. (Look up your own verses or use the following: 2 Corinthians 3:4-5; Psalm 119:129-130; Psalm 34:4-8, 15-19

5. In Isaiah 26:3 we read *"The steadfast of mind Thou wilt keep in perfect peace, because He trusts in Thee."*

   a. Write out how you would describe "perfect peace."

   b. Look up the word "steadfast" in a dictionary and write out what a steadfast mind would be like.

c. Now look up the following verses on trust. What should we not put our trust in and why?

Jeremiah 17:5-6

Proverbs 11:28

Jeremiah 7:4

2 Corinthians 1:9

6. Do you now see the importance of faithful, never-ending prayer in your life? Explain how it will help you as a mother right now.

Study Questions for Chapter Three

1. What do you see as the strengths and struggles of each of your children?

Name	Strengths	Struggles

2. Which struggle(s) frustrates you the most and why?

3. Can you see any pressure you're putting on your child that makes his or her struggles more difficult for both of you?

4. Using the section on "Ways to Refocus," what could you do to try and see this child as God sees him or her? What positive step will you take?

5. Read Colossians 1:9-12 and answer the following:

   a. What do we need to pray for and how will that affect our children? (vs. 9)

   b. What do we do with unfulfilled dreams according to these verses? (vs. 10)

c. Where do we get the strength to be what God intends us to be as mothers? (vs. 11) What are we promised?

6. Instead of worrying about broken dreams or unfulfilled expectations in our children, what does God say is important for us to focus on and why?

Matthew 6:19-21

1 Thessalonians 5:16-18, 24

7. What difference would this type of living make in our home? Really think about it.

STUDY QUESTIONS FOR CHAPTER FOUR

1. Reread the "What we can do" section of this chapter and write down one idea that might help your child.

2. Look at "How we can pray for our children" and choose three that you want to pray regularly for. List them in order of their importance in your child's life right now.

   a.

   b.

   c.

3. Think of one good choice you made this past week that you could share with your children.

4. Now write down a poor choice you made recently, and the consequences. Can you relate it on a level that your child(ren) will understand and learn from?

5. What usually causes you to lose heart with your children?

6. Now read again the verses in "Encouragement from God's heart to yours" in this lesson and list why we should never lose heart.

Which of the four verses brings you the most comfort?

7. In 2 Timothy 2:24-25 there are several personal qualities which God calls us to choose. Write each one and apply it to your situation.

    a.

    b.

    c.

    d.

    e.

STUDY QUESTIONS FOR CHAPTER FIVE

1. Describe the personality type of each of your children below.

2. Which child is the least like you? Why does this make it difficult to relate to or understand this child?

3. Go back and read James 1:2-5 in the "Encouragement" section. Which part of these verses do you need to believe and act on the most?

4. What "baby steps" have you seen in your child that you have squelched or ignored in your frustration?

5. What are God's instructions and words of encouragement to Joshua in chapter 1:5-9? Be specific about the instructions and decide how they apply to you as a mother.

   <u>Instructions:</u>

Application:

Encouragement:

Application:

6. After completing this study, write out a personal prayer thanking God for what He is teaching you or how He has comforted you.

STUDY QUESTIONS FOR CHAPTER SIX

1. List three ways that you might have described a "good mother" before you read this chapter. Then list three that you now feel are the most important qualities.

Before:

After:

2. As you think about "doing all in the name of Jesus" or representing Jesus in your children's lives, what has God spoken to you about?

3. Can you think of a time when your actions were right but your motives weren't? What was the result?

4. Is there something that you need to realize is "in the bank" with the Lord? How will that free you?

5. What can I learn from Jesus' attitude that I can ask God to help me apply to my life? Read Philippians 2:3-14 and fill in the chart below:

List examples of Christ's obedience and attitude.	How do I apply this in my daily life?
Vs. 3	
Vs. 4	

Vs. 5

Vs. 6

Vs. 7

Vs. 8

Vs. 12

Vs. 14

Which of these attitudes is most difficult for you?

Read verse 2:13 and explain how the above is possible.

STUDY QUESTIONS FOR CHAPTER SEVEN

1. When is it most difficult for you to show love to your child(ren)?

2. What do you now need to do to allow Jesus to love your child through you?

3. Look at I Corinthians 13 (a Mother's Paraphrase) again and list which area or areas in which the Holy Spirit is convicting you.

    a. What is the area?

    b. What will you do about it? (Be specific about the application.)

c. What verses can you find to help you with this?

4. How would you rate your discipline of your children right now?

	Poor	Fair	Great
	1	5	10
Consistency			
Patience			
Going through the steps of effective discipline			
Husband & Wife agree			
Results you see in kids			

5. In the "Training Children to Obey" section, which of the steps could you be more consistent in to bring about a heart change in your child?

6. Instead of being discouraged, look up Isaiah 41:10 and read it several times. Then take each phrase below and write out how you can apply it to loving and disciplining your children.

Do not fear:

I am with you:

Do not anxiously look around you:

I am your God:

I will strengthen you:

I will help you:

I will uphold you:

STUDY QUESTIONS FOR CHAPTER EIGHT

1. When do you personally feel most loved by God? (List several examples)

2. When do you feel the least loved by God? (List several examples)

3. Can you see how your perspective of God's love changes with your emotions? Is that focusing on truth? (Philippians 4:8)

4. What truths do you need to focus on from this lesson, so that you will consistently be aware of God's never-failing love for you, His child?

5. Study the verses below and write the promises and truths that you need to believe, no matter how you feel.

   a. Psalm 107:1,2

   b. Philippians 4:4-7

   c. Ephesians 3:18

d. Romans 11:33-36

e. Psalm 54:4

f. Luke 1:37

g. Ephesians 1:3-7

6. What do you want to praise and thank Him for right now?

STUDY QUESTION FOR CHAPTER NINE

1. Think about your expectations as a wife and mother for a moment. Which expectations cause you the most discouragement?

   With your mate:

   With your children:

   With yourself:

2. How does this affect your relationships with your family members?

3. How can you begin today to have more realistic expectations? Look at the list of what we can expect again.

Write one or two that you want to thank God for:

4. What expectations can you hold on to and claim in 1 Corinthians 15:57 and 58?

Verse 57 –

Verse 58 –

Why do you need to believe these?

5. Here are some more wonderful expectations we can have.

2 Timothy 2:11-12 –

2 Timothy 3:16-17 –

2 Timothy 4:18 –

1 Peter 1:6-8 –

2 Peter 1:3 –

James 1:5-6 –

STUDY QUESTIONS FOR CHAPTER TEN

1. Describe how you have experienced God's enabling grace in the past.

2. Since living with worry is rejecting God's grace, identify something you are worried about right now.

   How is this causing you to have a "divided mind?"

3. In order to experience God's grace on a daily basis, write out how you can take "baby steps" of obedience in your daily tasks. (example: "I will make sure to ask God for help before I begin my day.")

   a.

   b.

   c.

   d.

4. Think about the "mailbox principle" for a moment. Are you still holding on to a corner of the envelope? Specify what that corner is in the following areas:

In your marriage:

   I'm still hanging on to...

In your child:

   I'm still hanging on to...

In your friendships or extended family:
  I'm still hanging on to...

In your physical situation: (where you live, finances etc.)
  I'm still hanging on to...

5. What are you promised in Jeremiah 17:7-8, when you let go and put your whole trust in the Lord?

6. Are you ready to mail all of it?

To order additional copies of

Hope
and

Help
For a Mother's Heart

Please contact Carol Hopson at:
1015 Olive Crest Drive
Encinitas, CA 92024
(760) 942-6812

Other books by Carol Hopson include:
But God, I'm Tried of Waiting!
Peace in the Midst
My Day, His Way
But God… This Wasn't My Plan!